Krishen Khanna
Chola Migrations

Photography by Karan Khanna | Designed by Revanta Sarabhai | Produced and Published by Mapin Publishing | www.mapinpub.com

CONTEMPORARY INDIAN ARTISTS SERIES

Krishen Khanna

CHOLA MIGRATIONS

Norbert Lynton

Mapin Publishing

The Voyage of Migration

Fifty births
And rebirths
Won't make me forget
that crossing.
Long before men sought refuge
in imaginary lines,
passports hadn't been invented
Nor rules, self imposed, or otherwise,
fettered.

Frontiers were mountains as high
as heavens
And waves as high as the mountains.
By dim configuration of southern stars
to guide us,
The going wasn't easy I can tell you.
Climbing through cascading walls of water,
Mad chorus of winds
And serpentine columns of water
Struck like demons.
A terrible retribution for we
knew not what.

And those that didn't find their way
down the sea's gullet or the
ample bellies of fishes,
wound up on distant shores
with a white welcome of sea gulls.
The tumult of wind and water
yielding to the thick silence
of forests.

What quiet —
Silence unfolding
Screeching squirrels at play,
Monkey's chatter,
The peacock's plaint,
Hog's grunts
And the tiger's deafening roar.
Dark Patience stilling Time.

We wondered that we came
through never ending seas,
And forests holding terror,
Rocks that bled our feet,
Only to tend mute cattle
And to play the flute.

Krishen Khanna

First published in India in 2007 by
Mapin Publishing Pvt. Ltd.

Simultaneously published in the
United States of America in 2007 by
Grantha Corporation
77 Daniele Drive, Hidden Meadows
Ocean Township, NJ 07712
E: mapinpub@aol.com

Distributed in North America by
Antique Collectors' Club
East Works, 116 Pleasant Street, Suite 18
Easthampton, MA 01027
T: 1 800 252 5231 • F: 413 529 0862
E: info@antiquecc.com • www.antiquecollectorsclub.com

Distributed in the United Kingdom, Europe and the Middle East by
Art Books International Ltd.
Unit 200 (a), The Blackfriars Foundry, 156 Blackfriars Road
London, SE1 8EN UK
T: 44 207 953 7271 • F: 207 953 8547
E: sales@art-bks.com • www.art-bks.com

Distributed in Southeast Asia by
Paragon Asia Co. Ltd.
687 Taksin Road, Bukkalo, Thonburi
Bangkok 10600 Thailand
T: 66 2877 7755 • F: 2468 9636
E: info@paragonasia.com

Distributed in the rest of the world by
Mapin Publishing Pvt. Ltd.
10B Vidyanagar Society Part I
Usmanpura, Ahmedabad 380 014 INDIA
T: 91 79 2754 5390/2754 5391 • F: 91 79 2754 5392
E: mapin@mapinpub.com • www.mapinpub.com

ISBN: 978-81-88204-98-4 (Mapin)
ISBN: 978-0-944142-54-7 (Grantha)

Designed by Revanta Sarabhai / Mapin Design Studio
Edited by Diana Romany / Mapin Editorial
Processed by Reproscan
Printed in Malaysia

lead us to expect delicate chamber music, he gives us the fullest orchestration laid open to his vision and skill with this apparently so limited instrument. In the best hands, minimal means often produce maximal results. Between the darkest and lightest areas in the mural comes a wealth of lines and areas of tone, spacious here, concentrated and accented there. The effect of his carefully modulated tones struck me as bringing his mural close to relief sculpture. It so happens that Mahabalipuram, just south of Chennai, has the world's largest stone relief, dating back to the time before the Cholas became the rulers of Tamil Nadu: a vast stone frieze, twenty-seven metres long and crowded with deities and other figures, with birds and elephants and other animals. Khanna surely knew this remarkable work. He had, of course, always made drawings on paper, and it is striking that several of his paintings of that early time but also later, come close to being monochromatic, often in dark grey or black oil or acrylic on an off-white canvas.

The theme he chose for his mural is historical rather than mythical, celebrating the outgoing activities of the Chola, not the richness and beauty of what they established at home. He offers us a vision of families and animals on the land, going about their various tasks amid palm trees and rocks, including carrying goods from the ships, and then the ships and the men on them, venturing forth into heavy seas. The ships he studied in a bas relief in Borabadur in Indonesia, converting what he saw into his vivid idiom of light and dark patches, done almost as if the black were there already and he drew over it, or erased it, to create white forms that are the decks of the ships, their masts and even the voyagers themselves. The scenes on dry land show some things pencilled in firmly—a tree trunk, for instance—but many of the figures are delivered in white or smudged pale grey, while the spaces between them are marked with black. (In the carved reliefs that helped Khanna develop his vision, the projecting parts appear lighter in tone than the shadowed spaces between them.) The ships and seas are formed as two great waves of energy and action against a mostly light sky, and it is striking that the scenes on land are also composed in arched units, as though those at home too have their venturesome lives, though in safer conditions.

The figures here are strong, majestic even, once we accept this negative tonal idiom, and notice how the leaves of palm trees, or a dramatic black bird, can give this world its rhythmical cohesion.

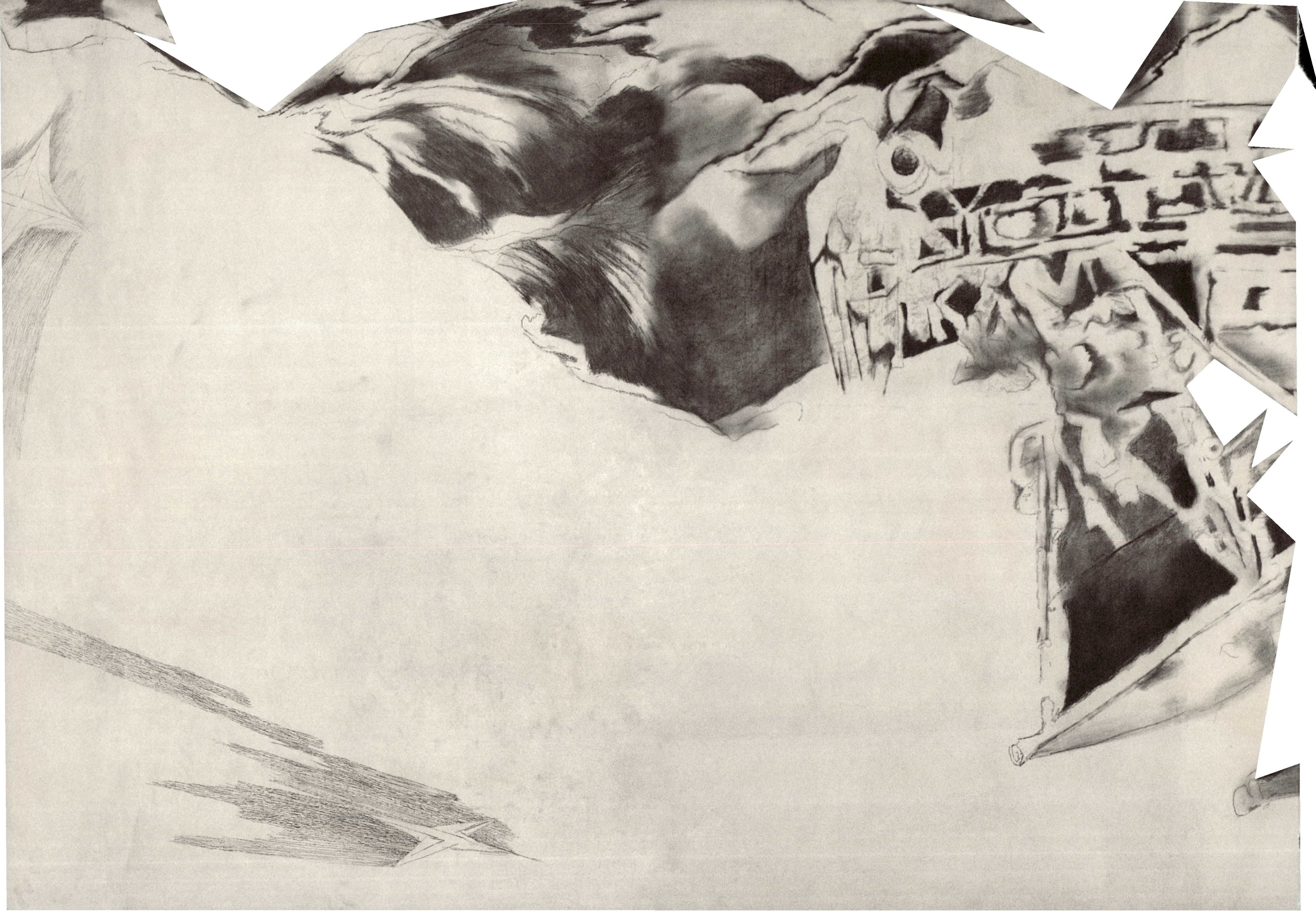

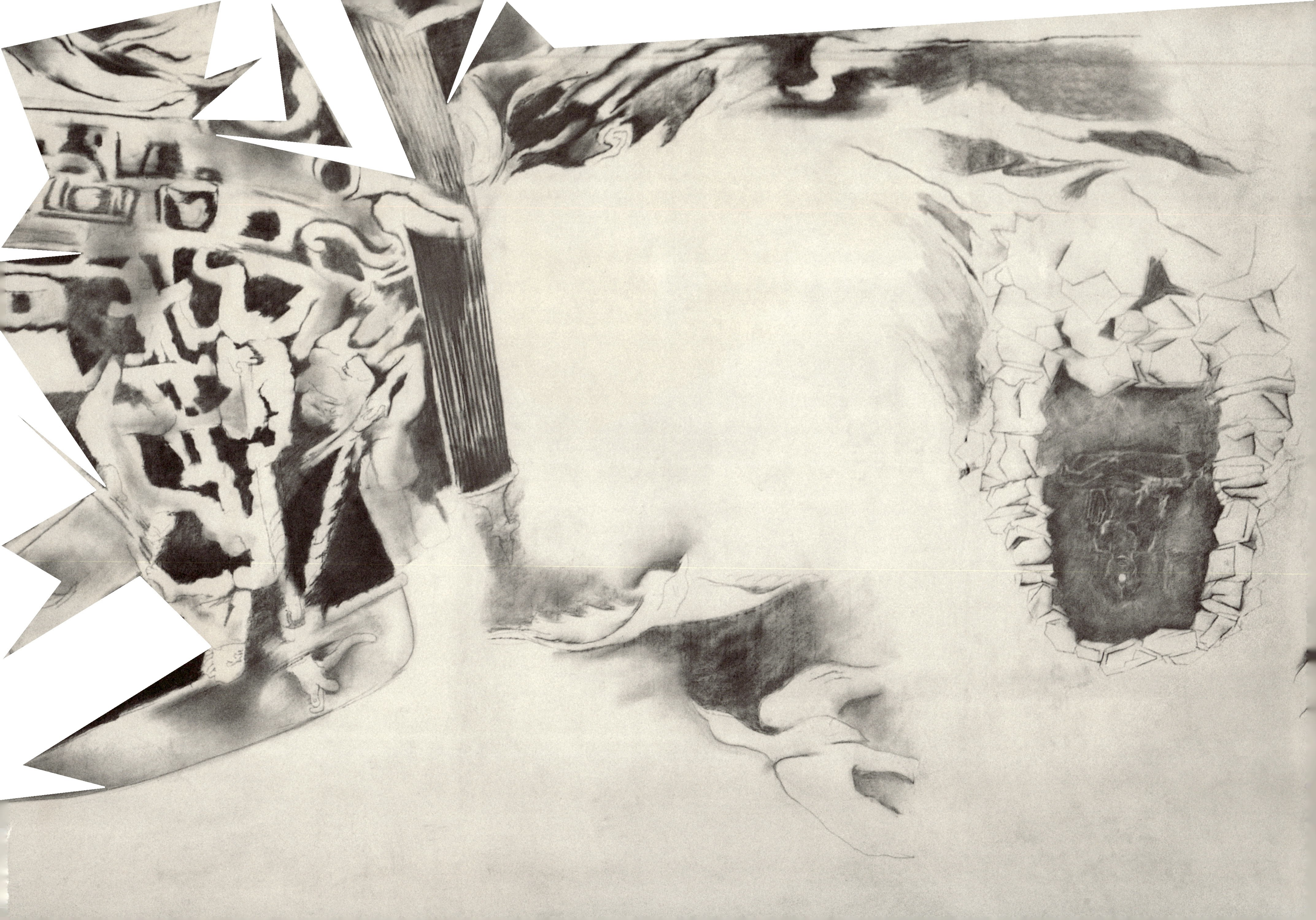

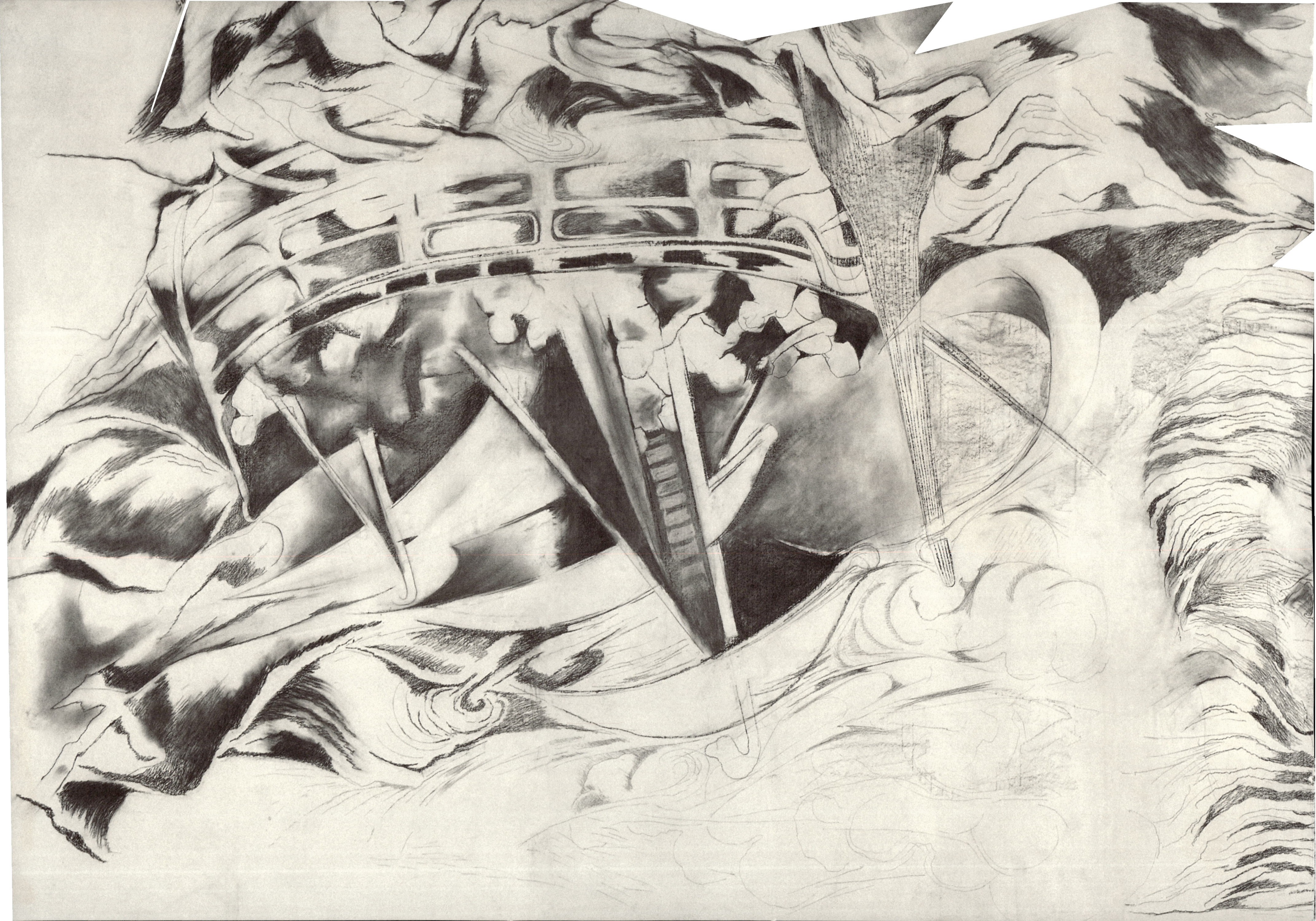

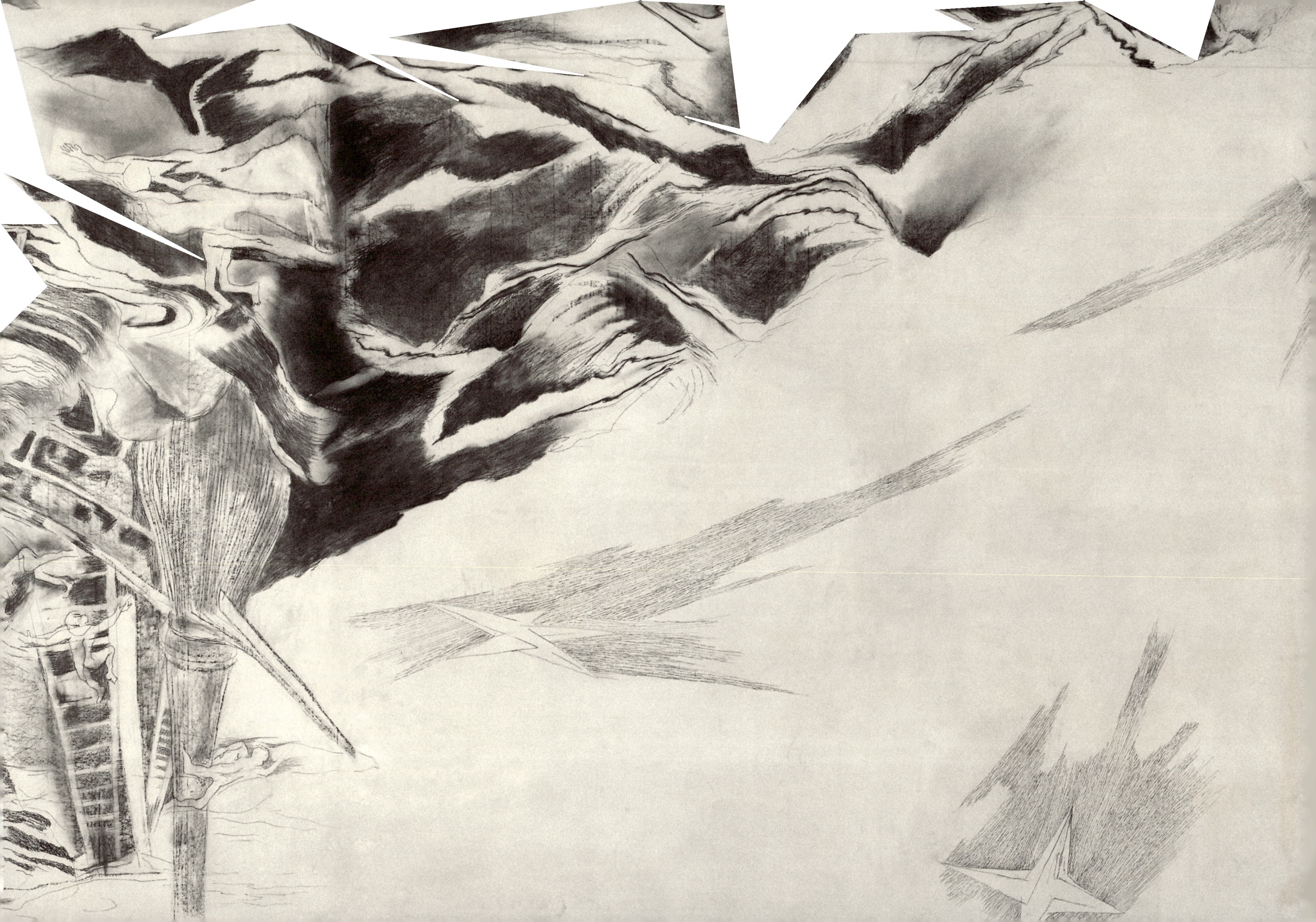

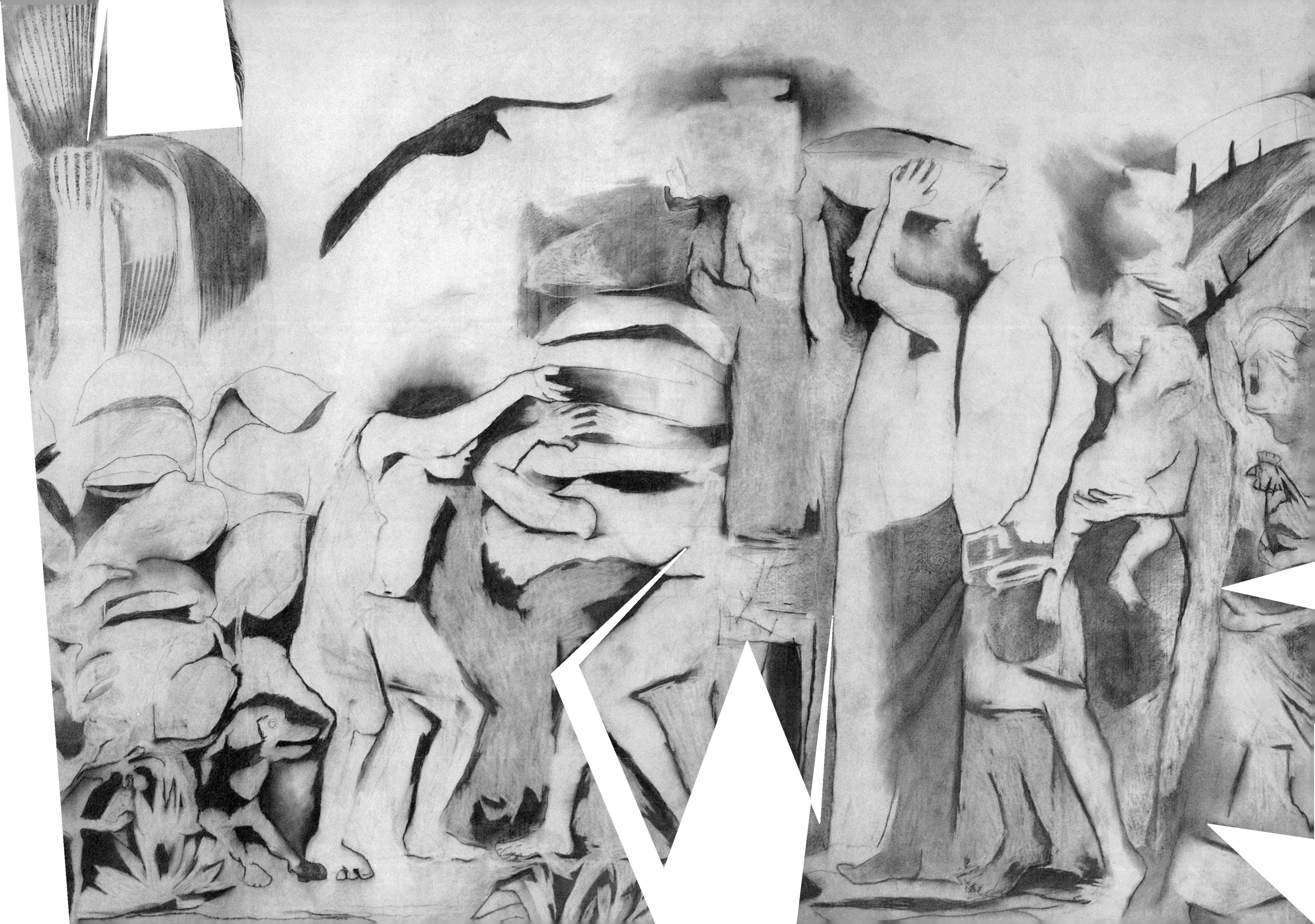

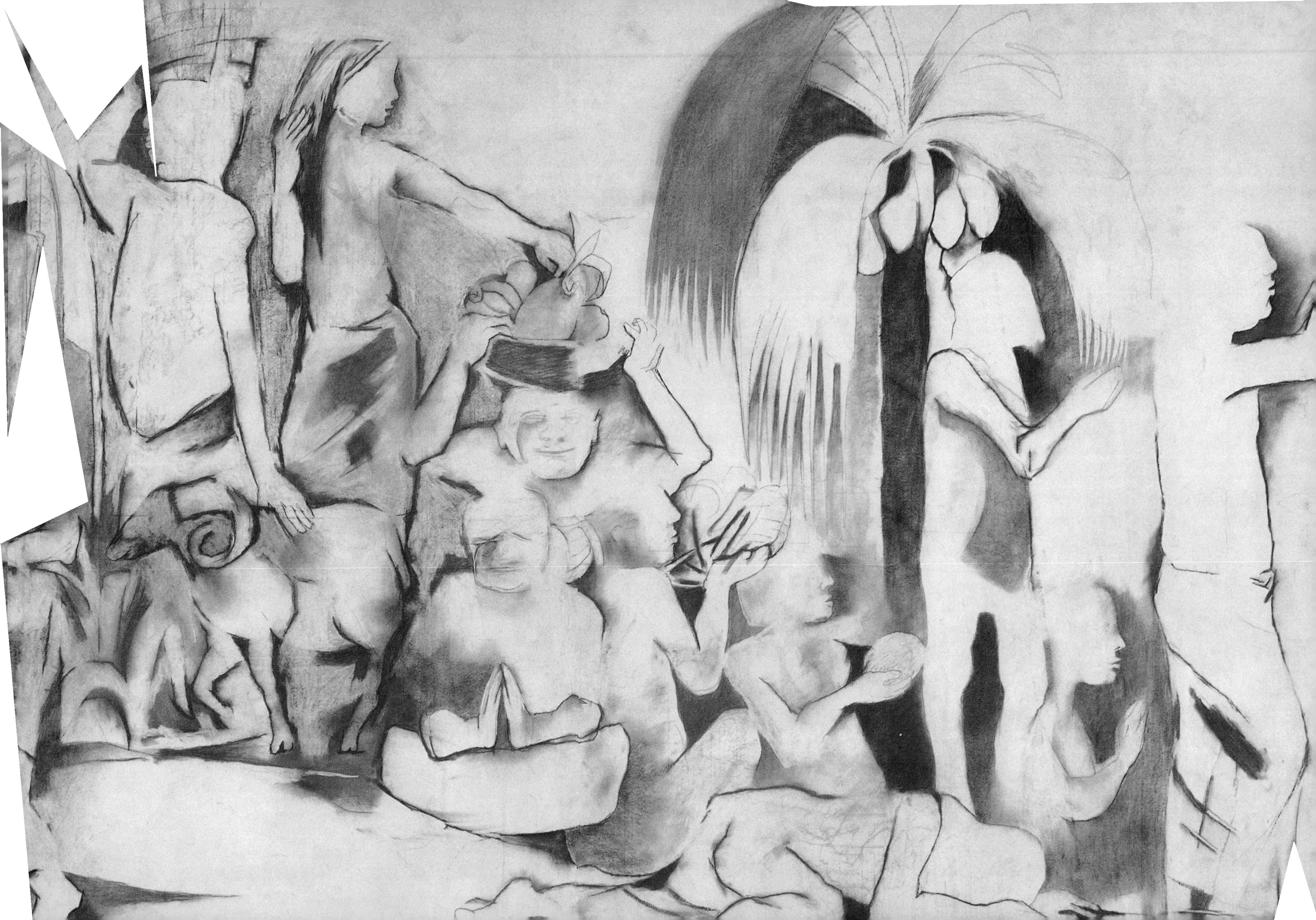

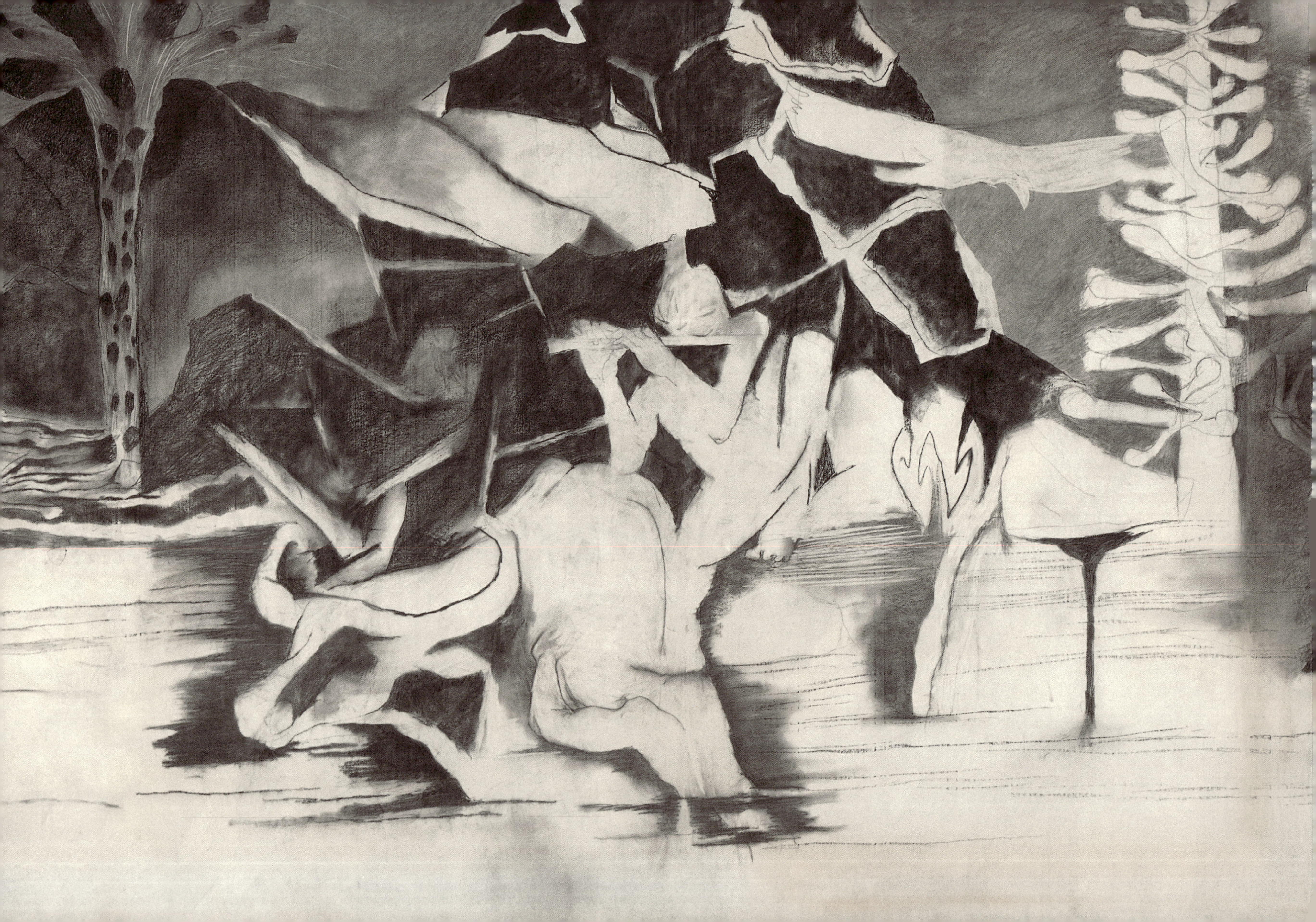

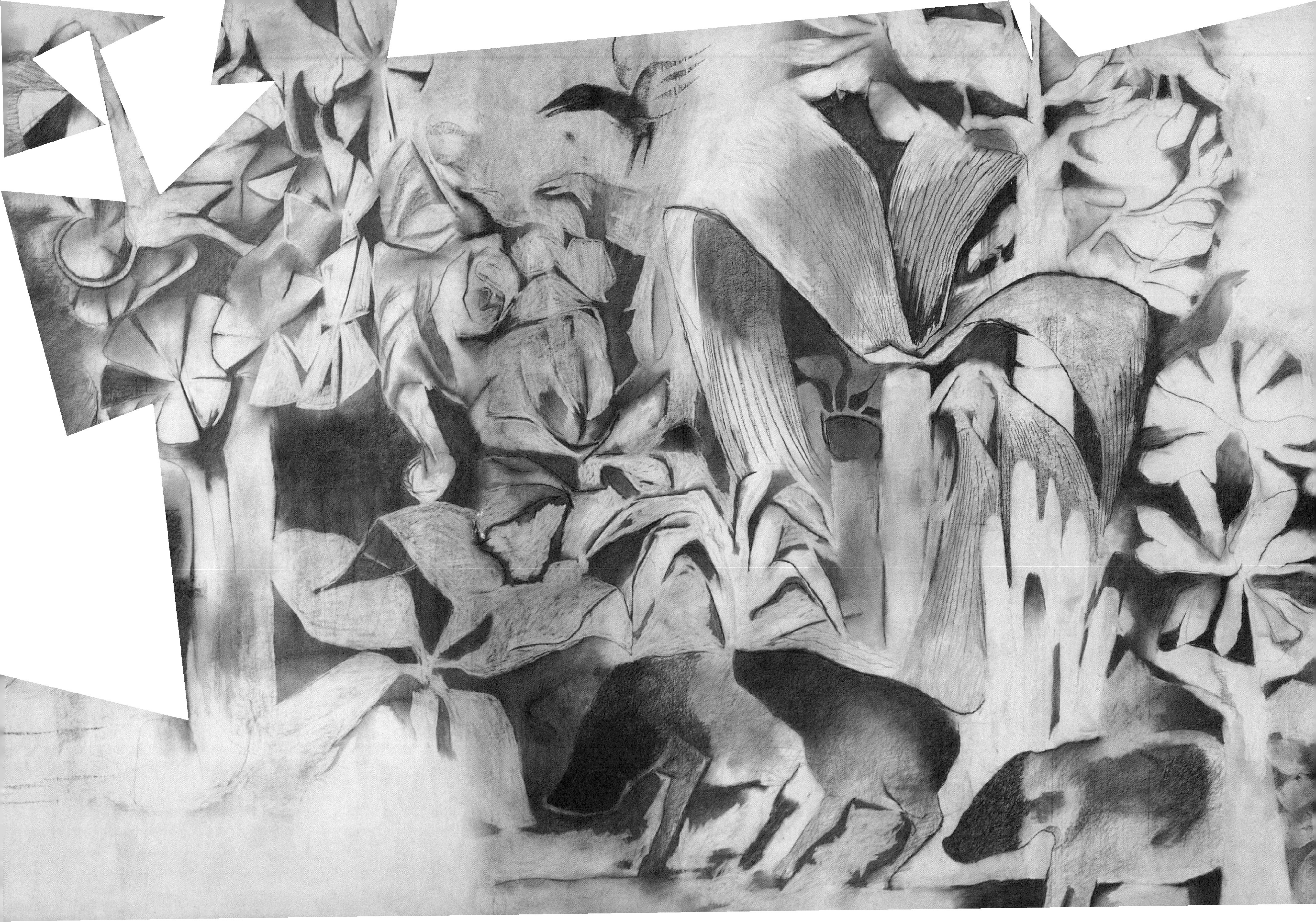